Silent Healing

By

Michael Anderson

Text copyright © 2018 Michael Anderson & Living Large Press

All Rights Reserved

Dedication

To the poetry lovers

and

non-judgmentals

Preface

I am always leery of writing the preface because I am afraid of forgetting someone to thank; So many people go into and contribute to a project and they probably don't even know it. But I will try.

Thank you to Ms. Lucas, my 11th grade English teacher. I was such a poor student that when I scored a 100 on a vocabulary test once she made me retake it because she thought I cheated. However, she was the first one to encourage me to write.

My mom, of course, because she did what any good mother does: told me that what I wrote is good and that she was proud of me. Hopefully she continues to rest in peace.

To Rebecca, the subject of the poem, *10 Words of Pain* and the inspiration of many poems that will be contained in the next book. I still haven't met you or have seen you in person, but one day….

And finally, to my family and friends, past and present. You have all contributed in some way to the inspirations that come and eventually live on in written form. Without you, there would be no me, no writing, no books. Thank you!!

Part I
#thelifeofmichael

"Have you ever cheated?" she asked.
"Only in my mind." I responded.
"With whom?"
"Take your pick."

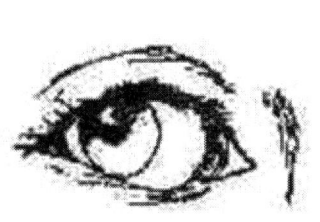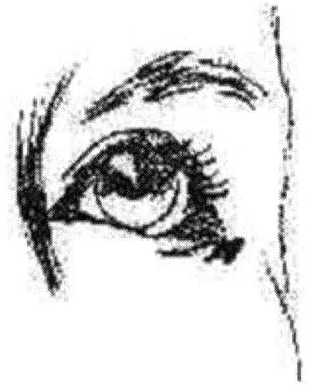

I once asked God
If he punishes us for sin.
*"The knowing you sinned and
Living with that
Is punishment enough."* he answered.
    ----Sometimes I think he lied.

I sometimes wonder
If I have it worse than others…
If I should continue to carry
The burden of past transgressions
Like a dead soldier being brought
Back home on his shield.
  Because somedays I feel
  That what I feel and experience
  Will never end…
  The pain of loss
  The guilt of wrongdoings
  "Am I a good parent?"
  "Am I a good spouse?"
  "Am I a good friend?"
  "Am I truly the professional I think and project that I am?"
  "Am I?"
My constant questioning
Wears on me like tire rubber
Magically disappearing over time
Until the tire is bald and
Unusable and must be
Discarded in hopes that
Some savior will retread it
So that tens of thousands of more miles
Can be gained from its use.
  But then I remember…
  And I always remember
  Because the mind plays those
  Fucked up types of games with you…
  That what is happening now,

That what I am experiencing or
Putting myself through
Won't happen or last forever, because
My *Now* is not an
Ending.

I read once where a professor
Asked his Quantum Physics
Class to describe the chair
He had placed in the front
Of the room.

This question was the only question
On the final exam.
There was only one *"A"*
And it was from
A student who answered the question
With a question: *What Chair?*

I understood that for one simple reason:
I understand that things exist,
Even if we don't seem them,
Just as things don't exist
Even if we do.

Things change, even
If they are one way
Now.
       ---Even people, whether they realize it or not.

**Yes. I still dance.
Just not with you.**
---Unfortunately, or not.

Your opened legs
Welcomed me home
And I willingly
French-kissed
Its door.

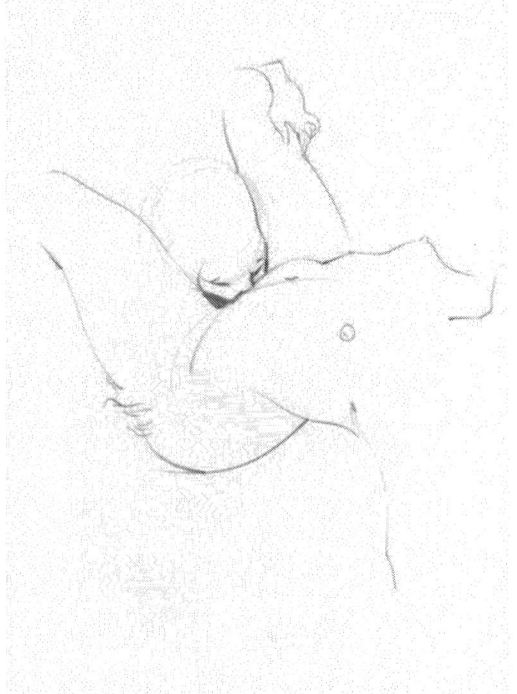

I just read a
Black woman's
Blogpost titled,
"The Anger of the White Male Lie"

In the post she said,
"Somebody needs to stop
Telling these white boys that
They can be anything they put
Their minds to."

I thought about this
For a while, and
Came up with a response:
"Why?"

I drink coffee
Like most people
Drink water.

I wish I could
Love someone like
I do coffee.

You're wearing flip-flops!
Yes?
It's 40° outside!
Yes?
Why?
Because my son
Is wearing my shoes.

Stereotypes

A pick-up truck parked beside us.
A barefoot man with jeans,
A Red-Man tobacco baseball cap,
And no shirt
Got out.

So did an overweight,
Barefoot woman wearing
Cut-off jean shorts and a
Man's wife-beater
Tee-shirt.

And so did a small child
Wearing nothing but a diaper.

"THAT" exclaimed the girl
From New Jersey, *"is EXACTLY
How I pictured Alabama to be."*

I often wish
For more time to read
But that would take away
From my time
Spent thinking.

My first love
Is myself and
I never left.

My second love
Is the pen and
She has returned.
        ---And I still Love her.

*"Why is it so hard to follow
My first instinct?"* she asked.

Why does "C" come after "B"
And
"B" come after "A?" I retorted

"I don't know."

Because that's just the way it is.

Life doesn't reward you for just participating.

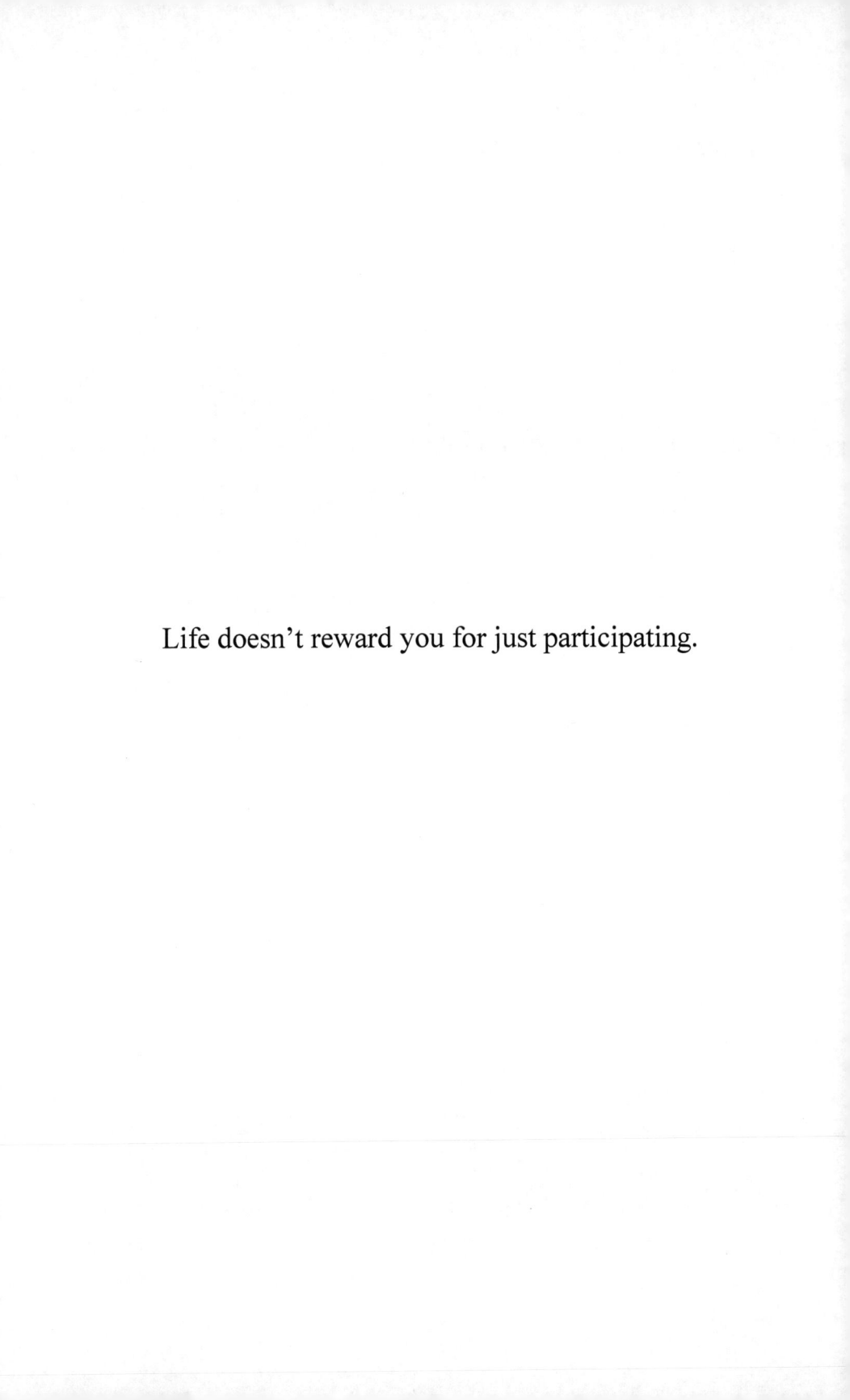

Is *"is,"* is?

Whoever first said
*"You can't have your cake
And eat it too"* is dumb.

What's the purpose, after all,
Of having cake if you can't eat it?
	---Unanswerable questions.

"Life is short." She said.
"But it's the longest thing you
Will ever do!" I exclaimed.

Her look told me
She was silently calling
Me an asshole.

I bumped into a lady recently.
"Oh. I'm sorry!" I said.
"No! you're fine!" she responded.
"Why, thank you!" I replied.

She walked away confused.
    ---LOL

Marcus Aurelius said, "Remember…
in life your duties are the sum of
individual acts."

Thus, find clarity in the
Simplicity of doing.

1.
I knew,
As I walked out of the room
After saying my goodbyes
And expressing my love
That the next time I saw my mom
She would be dead.

2.
I was dreaming…
"Mom!"
"Mom!"
"It's Michael.
Can you hear me?"
Yes. I can hear you.
"How are you? Are you ok?"
Yes. But they only let me eat eggs here.
"You have a visitor.
Your nephew, Steve, is here."

The dream ended
As the phone
Began to ring.

3.
"Hello?"
She's gone, dude.
"When?"
About 15 minutes ago.
"Ok. Thanks for calling."

4.
"They" say *forgive and forget*
But I am having a hard time doing
Either because my brother left
Hospice and our mother
Died alone, with no family around.
5.
The worst part of that day
Were the people…
The people from my old church
Telling me how much
My mom meant to them
And how good of a friend
She was to them
And how much
They loved her

Yet…

They hadn't seen her in years,
Decades…
They never called
They never visited.

So yeah.
The same people who took
The church from my mom
Was telling me such bullshit,
And I didn't know these
"God fearing" Christians could
Be such hypocrites.

The worst part of that day
Were the people…
    ---No doubt.

6.
I didn't speak
At my mom's funeral
Because I was afraid
Of what I might say.

I call a spade a spade
And the chapel was full
Of them that day.
One morning,
I went to the store with
Bed head hair
Non-brushed teeth
Morning breath
Lounge pants
Flip-flops
No underwear
And my cleanest dirty shirt.
    ---The Walmart Effect

My dad was old school
And would say, "Nothing
Comes easy."

And I grew up
Believing that, until
It did.

My son loves a black girl.
Well…Jamaican, actually.
Is that okay? He asked me once.
"Does she make you happy?" I asked him back
Yes.
"Then it's ok."

The first time
I touched a breast
I was in the 7th grade.
I didn't touch the nipple,
Just the top, exposed portion
Of the breast.

She made fun of me
Because I wouldn't
"go further."

We broke up.

The universe has
A weird way of letting
You know how it feels.

I failed a professional
Certification exam today.
When I got into my car
And turned on the radio
Beck's song, *Loser*
Was playing.
       ---REALLY?!?!

Emoji Poetry

Rock

Paper

Scissors

SHOOT!

I know a girl
Who has anxiety
And is a depressed drug addict.

Her addiction takes her
To the houses of
Strangers
Where she buys drugs
With money
Pussy
And her mouth.

And when she doesn't have
Any drugs
She breaks her fingers
So the doctor will give her
Pain meds, or
She takes her pets
To the vet
So they can get
Pain meds, then
She takes them.

She's getting married
To her gay
Best friend from high school,
Who is also an addict
And a felon in three
Counties.

All of this

At the age of 25,
And to spite her parents.

I want to help her
But I can't because
She won't help herself first.

PART II
Silent Healing

The wind gusts
The leaves tumble
And travel to places
They know not where.

I want to be a leaf.

The first time SHE left
She went to work
After our first
Weekend together.
I cried because
I would miss her, and
I loved her.

The LAST time I left
I went back home
Because she loved
Someone else
And wasn't leaving where
She grew up…her home.
I cried not just because
I would miss her, and
Still loved her.

But because I fucked up
And knew
I would never see her
Hold her
Taste her
Hear her
Again.

10 Words of Pain

When you were born,
She wouldn't let me
See you.

The loneliest feeling for me
Is knowing
You are upstairs
And I am downstairs
Yet we are both
Okay with that.

She rode me as
My passed-out brother
And his not passed out wife
"slept" in the other bed
In the hotel room.

And there were no words.
Just quiet
Rhythmic
Slow
Soft
Smooth
Lovemaking
That would make any
Rolling wave jealous.

I poured some pepper
Into a glass where
The oil had risen
To the top of the water.
At the first pepper flake
The oil rushed to the edges
Of the glass,
Getting as far away from
The pepper as possible.

I sometimes feel like pepper
Because you act like oil
When I crawl into bed
With you.

Why do I care
When you don't?
Why do I love
When you won't?
Why do I see
When you sleep?
Why do I care
What you think?
      ---I don't, really

Hold me,
And let me
Fall asleep with
My finger in
Your belly-button
Like I did when
We were first dating.
    ---I want to feel safe.

People lie…

Yet we continue
To live each day
Believing that others
Have the same
Good heart as ours.

I don't understand
Your reluctance at
Being honest.

Just fucking tell me
So I will
Stop guessing.

I can hear your
Silence
With each breath taken
Each glance stolen
With each empty
Touch.

Emptiness…as
From a shattered glass
Sending shards
Of my life
Racing across the
Empty canvas

Longing,
Waiting to be painted
Not knowing the paint
Has dried up
And the brush bristles
Have shed themselves
Like dandelion thistles
Being blown
By the wind.

Thoreau once said,
"It's not what you look at
That matters. It's what
You see."

But I don't see
Anything
When I look at you
    ---Is that sad?

20 years later
She asked the $10,000 question:
Why did you leave?

I gave her
The $5 answer:
To save you from me.

I continued…

I left because
I was selfish
And a drunk
A whore
A liar
Cheater
And thief.

Not because of you.

Some days,
I want to sleep
until I feel better mentally.

But when I sleep
Too long
I hurt physically.

Then I must decide
If the mental pain of
Being awake
Is worse than the physical pain
Of sleeping.

People love to ask,
"Are you ok?"
Me, on the outside: *Yes.*
Me, on the inside: *I am sorry for*
Being such a mess.

"I DON'T UNDERSTAND! she cried,
*"WHY OTHERS KEEP TAKING
ADVANTAGE OF ME!"*

"Because you keep putting them first." I replied

"And what the FUCK is wrong with THAT?"

"You have taught them that YOU come second."

Loneliness…

The ULTIMATE poverty.

What are you doing?
Pondering.
Pondering, what?
What I am supposed to do
When someone I love
Becomes a stranger.

Just smile
And no one will
Disturb you.

*But I am so empty.
Can't you hear my heart
Crying?*

I am NOT lonely!
But the first sign of
Alcoholism is denial.
So!
So…you are denying
You are lonely.
NO, I AM NOT!!!

Epilogue

Someone asked me once why I was offering this book for free on Kindle. The answer was a no-brainer for me: it didn't cost me anything to write it, so why should it cost something to read it? My hope is that you enjoyed reading it as much as I enjoyed writing it.

So I get asked often, "What's next?" I have so many ideas on books that it sometimes gets overwhelming thinking about them. But I can assure you that the next two books will be Volume 2 of the Living Large Daily Tidbits and a second poetry book. After that, I can't say. I just hope that if you have hung with me this far, that you will be there in the future. Without you there would be no me, no writing, no books. Why create if you can't share, right?

I am grateful for you, and I am humbled that you took time out of your busy day and life to read this book. Having a family, a full-time job, and a side gig as a local school board member, I understand how precious our 24-hours are. Knowing you took time out of YOUR 24-hours to indulge me and my writings is beyond fathomable. But I am glad you did. And I love you for it.

Finally, I am always eager to connect with new people and hear your stories, so please feel free to connect with me at the following:

Facebook: LivingLarge19

Twitter: @livinglarge19

Instagram: @living.large19

Made in the USA
Lexington, KY
02 November 2018